A light in the dark of night,
a comforting hand on the shoulder
in time of trouble,
a guide to one who has lost his way.
A "spirit lifter" is all of these.
Let Virginia Whitman show you
how you can provide the help that
others need from time to time.
In these pages she gives the
inspiration and the practical
know-how so you can
BE A SPIRIT LIFTER!

Be a Spirit Lifter

Virginia Whitman

ACCENT BOOKS

Denver, Colorado

MEMBER OF
EVANGELICAL CHRISTIAN
PUBLISHERS ASSOCIATION

ACCENT BOOKS
A division of Accent-B/P Publications, Inc.
12100 W. Sixth Avenue
P.O. Box 15337
Denver, Colorado 80215

Liabrary of Congress Catalog Card Number: 77-93251

ISBN 0-916406-97-0

Contents

1
Everyone Needs
Encouragement

Mike leaned over and gave Tricia a perfunctory kiss as he rose from the breakfast table to leave for work. As he went out the door he knew he should have paused to help her sop up the milk Timmie had spilled. She'd had a tough time of it the past three weeks, but he couldn't get his mind off things at the plant. The way business was going, he might get a lay off notice any day.

Tricia was thinking of the same possibility as Mike went out the door. *I should have sent him away with a smile,* she thought as she wiped up the spilled milk, *but what is there to smile about?*

She'd been housebound for the past three weeks while the children, one after another, had had the measles. It had prevented her from giving her mother the support she needed while Tricia's father was in the hospital for minor surgery. And now, this morning, Tricia felt as if she were coming down with a nasty cold. She wanted to weep but the ringing phone made her brace herself. With a sigh she answered it. It was her best friend.

"Oh, Dottie," Tricia confessed, "I'm so blue I wonder if things will ever get any better! To top everything else off, I'm afraid I'm coming down with a cold."

"Maybe not," Dottie told her. "I know you're having a lot of trials, but try to encourage yourself like David did. You know, he told himself, "Why art thou cast down, O my soul? . . . Hope thou in God" (Psalms 42:5).

"Say it over three times," Dottie urged Tricia, "and put the emphasis on a different word each time like this: *Hope* thou in God. Hope *thou* in God. Hope thou in *God.* I'll be praying for Him to lift your spirits," she promised.

If depression could be gauged with instruments or by laboratory analysis as blood pressure, cholesterol level, or insulin deficiency can, its presence would probably be evident in every person at some time. With most of us, it would occur as a passing mood; with some, it is a chronic state; with others, a critical condition. Because it is so frequently present in individuals, it has been termed the "common cold of psychiatry."

That it has for years been our nation's number one illness supports such a conclusion. Moreover, the World Health Organization reports that, daily, about 1,000 persons commit suicide and 10,000 attempt it. Discouragement is the leading cause in these cases. The National Institute of Mental Health in Washington, D.C. is quoted as saying, "We have noticed an increase, a decided increase, in suicidal deaths due to financial pressure and unemployment."

Persons with this degree of emotional disturbance usually need professional help, but over against that "few" are *countless* numbers of depressed persons who could be benefited by spirit lifters which you and I can provide for them.

The results of depression vary in depth and scope from a passing unhappiness to a neurotic state in which, as previously mentioned, suicide is considered or attempted. In between are diverse reactions, such as irritability, inefficiency, even illness. Headaches, nausea, bowel trouble, loss of appetite or other symptoms may appear as a result of depression.

In most cases, the factors that induce depression are ordinary problems of life which any of us may encounter. For instance, loss of self esteem: A wife downgrades her husband in the presence of his in-laws; a teacher ridicules a pupil in the midst of his peers; a supervisor reprimands an employee before his fellow-workers.

Or depression may occur because of frustrating circumstances—a situation with which one cannot cope. The victim of this situation may "ballon" the odds against himself, and as a result of his distorted perspective, become discouraged. As an example, a businessman lost a customer account he valued. Without taking into consideration what a small percentage of his total business volume it represented, he became unduly morose about it.

A person can become discouraged when he seems to have the least reason to be. Sometimes those who, in the eyes of others, have everything in the world to be glad about, become very depressed.

Encountering a number of abrasive people one after another may result in despondency. Where only one such incident would have been taken in stride, a succession of them may overwhelm.

Natalie asked the postman about a package she was expecting. His curt, "It'll be delivered just as soon as it gets here," disconcerted her. A few minutes later when she answered the phone she was greeted with, "Why weren't you at the meeting last night?" Later when she stopped at a service station on her way to the supermarket, the operator chided her with, "Your tires show that you're using your brakes too much." When she took her groceries out of the basket at the cash register, the checker snapped, "Why didn't you put a divider between this lady's groceries and yours?"

As she drove back home, Natalie recalled all these experiences. *My goodness!* she told herself, *I can't do anything right,* and she tail-spinned into a period of discouragement.

Often it is the cumulative effect of circumstances which throws one out of balance emotionally. Whenever that occurs and we encounter a person in a state of dejection, our *ministry of encouragement* may come to the rescue. Every day, by God's leading and enablement, each one of us has it within his power to become a spirit lifter. Let's note the opportunities and means that may be ours.

2
Spouses Can Be Encouraged

Michelle could tell the minute Rick opened the door that all was not well. Instead of a glad smile, his countenance was glum, the corners of his mouth sagged, his eyes were lustreless.

"Hi, honey!" she greeted him. "It's sure nice to have you home. Hasn't it been a lovely day? I believe spring has finally sprung," she laughed, searching his face for an up-beat response.

There was none. His shoulders drooped as he headed for the bathroom. He washed up in silence with no running comments on the day's events, as was normally the case.

She put the hot dishes on the table, wishing she had prepared a tastier meal which might have lifted his spirits. It sometimes did. As they sat down, he asked her to express their thanks. Usually, he did so.

Along with her spoken words, she sent up a silent, quickie prayer: "Oh, Lord, You know what's the matter. Help me to be patient until he's ready to talk, and then help me to say the right thing and give him comfort or whatever he needs."

As she passed the food she reported on her day, omitting anything of a negative nature, emphasizing the positive aspects. She subtly tried to draw him out. Whatever his trouble, airing it would help. He volunteered nothing until he had finished a scant helping of everything.

"You're not eating much," she told him. "I'm sorry my menu didn't ring the bell tonight."

"The food's good enough. I'm just not hungry."

"What's the matter?" she ventured. "Is something bothering you?"

A frown wrinkled his face and it was a few seconds before he responded. Michelle held her breath, suspecting he was weighing whether or not to unload.

"The Liggett order didn't reach them by the date specified and they called Mr. Baxter and raised sand about it. Of course he jumped on me. You remember that was the order they phoned in and I was late getting home because I took it down to the main post office before I came home to make sure it would go right out. . . ."

"Did you tell Baxter that?" Doesn't he realize how undependable the postal service is any more?"

Every husband has his vocational discouragements. It is part of the wife's responsibility to help him cope with them, to push self to the background, at least until his need of heartening has been met.

That begins with being alert and sensitive to his mood. Affording a sympathetic ear is, of course, in order. Such comments as, "You ought to have known". . . or "I've told you many a time . . ." are to be avoided.

Constructive suggestions, if offered, should be tactfully and sweetly made. Ministering to a husband's physical comfort often bolsters his morale.

The economic responsibilities which a husband bears are often a source of discouragement to him. Marcia and Jim were spending a Sunday afternoon at home—a rare occurrence. Marcia was reading and Jim had been sitting at the desk, pencil in hand. Suddenly he threw it down, sighed and shook his head, apparently forgetting that Marcia was in the room with him.

Marcia laid down her book and, crossing over to her husband, placed her hands gently on his shoulders.

"Why the deep sigh, dear? Is something troubling you?"

Jim's head bowed in dejection. It was a moment before he answered, and when he spoke, his voice registered discouragement.

"It's just no use. There's simply no way to do it!"

"Do what?"

"Make our income keep up with inflation. Every month it's the same battle over again, only worse each time. There's the raft of monthly payments—mortgage on the house, installments on the car, allotment for the hospital bill — all the regular debits on our budget.

"Then there's always something unexpected, like that leak in the bathroom plumbing. And all the utilities— water, electricity, and phone—are going up again. It's beyond me. I don't know what to do. Up until now I've managed some way each time, but now I'm beat. I tell you, *I'm beat!*" He jumped to his feet and strode out the door. Marcia was genuinely alarmed and dropped to her knees.

"Dear God," she prayed, "take care of Jim and calm him down. Show me how to help him. If I'm at fault or could do better with the part of our income I handle, show me about that."

She went to the door and peeked out to see where Jim had gone. Relieved, she noted he had crossed the street and was talking to Ted Shelton.

Maybe he'll cheer Jim up, she thought.

Had she known the facts, the situation was the reverse. After complimenting Ted on the neat job of hedge trimming he was doing, Jim had innocently asked, "Are you making lots of car sales these days?"

Before Ted replied, he reached high up and savagely snipped off a sprout which towered above those around it. Jim was not aware of the symbolical significance of the gesture, although it did register that there seemed to be more vehemence to the act than was called for.

"Business is rotten," Ted replied. "I don't know why I chose to be a salesman. The manager is after you day in and day out, saying, 'We've got to meet our quota. The month is nearly gone. You're falling behind. Get on the ball. The boss has his heart set on winning that trip to Hawaii. His wife is bugging him about it.'" Ted mimicked, then went on.

"I go over my prospect list again. I make endless phone calls. I get a guy to come in. I work on him tooth and toenail with all the angles I can muster. I get him just about ready to close the deal, and what happens?"

Jim had no idea.

"That goat from the outfit across the street walks over and brazenly proposes, 'I've got a better value than this to offer you. Come on over and see it. Then you can come back here if you still want to . . .'"

"That would make a fellow mad," Jim sympathized. "What did you say?"

"I was too flabbergasted to say anything."

"Did the prospect come back?"

Ted shook his head.

"Why don't you call him again just to be sure he bought the other fellow's car?"

"I'm too discouraged," Ted explained. "The boss saw him leave and go across the street. He rode me about letting him slip through my fingers."

"That was tough," Jim admitted, "but never say die. Don't give up. Things are never so bad that they could not be worse." And then he thought to himself, *is it he or I that needs to be told that?*

Husbands do indeed encounter economic difficulties and competitive pressures that are more than sufficient to dishearten them. As James Collier pointed out in a *Woman's Day* article some years ago, every morning the breadwinner sets out to walk a tightrope over an abyss of possible failure. Wives and others need to be ready to encourage him.

It wasn't until Sharon attended a seminar for executives' wives that she realized the many temptations to which her husband might be subject.

"Did you ever consider the provocations your husband has which might cause him to be less than his best?" the seminar leader asked. "And yet you are always prodding him about getting ahead and winning a promotion.

"For instance, there are temptations to dishonesty. They range all the way from trivialities like using company stamps for personal mail to embezzling large sums of money.

"There are temptations to blow his top and tell off an unreasonable superior who really has it coming; yet, to do so might jeopardize his job or chance for advancement.

"Or there may be unsolicited enticements to infidelity, because no matter how carefully a company screens its employees, there will be an unscrupulous female now and then. Your husband may not yield to any of these or to other temptations that confront him, but he can be discouraged by them. Are you prepared to cheer him on and make resistance seem worthwhile? Or do you add to his discouragement until he throws up his hands and says, 'What's the use?'"

Maybe temptations account for Bob seeming so discouraged sometimes, Sharon concluded.

Wives, no less than husbands, need encouragement. The Bible even gives specific instructions about it: "When a man hath taken a new wife, he shall not go out to war, neither shall he be charged with any business: but he shall be free at home one year, and shall *cheer up* his wife which he hath taken" (Deuteronomy 24:5).

Seldom can a newlywed husband take a year off all at one time to cheer up his wife, but he *can* offer as much or more time in installments. Every evening when a man comes home from work he can recognize the possibility that his wife needs encouragement.

When Jerry came home one midweek evening, he noted that Diane was not groomed as meticulously as usual. When she said, "Hi!" there was no lilt in her voice. She even suffered his kiss of greeting in an indifferent manner.

"What's the score today?" he questioned.

"Nothing much, same old six and seven," she replied.

"Anything go wrong? Did the kids get into mischief?"

She shook her head and merely said, "They're already in bed."

"Maybe I should have asked what went right," he opined.

Diane shrugged her shoulders. Jerry was puzzled. Something was evidently amiss, but he was not astute enough to analyze what. He tried reporting on his day, but his wife's lack of interest stumped him.

"I don't understand," he said at last. "What has happened?"

"That's just it. *Nothing ever happens.* It's always the same—morning, noon, and night, day after day. *You* get out and meet different people and see different places, but all *I* see is these four walls. I cook the same three meals, I wash the same clothes, I go through the same routine, the same unrewarding repetition daily. And I don't see any prospect of change—at least for years and years. I'm utterly discouraged!" and she commenced to cry.

Or just the opposite may be the cause of a wife's discouragement. Because they were a one-car family, Kathy had to take Mark to work, get back to fix breakfast and see the children off to school. Some days she then had to chauffeur her mother-in-law to the market, go to the Laundromat, have the car serviced, take their daughter for her music lesson, or pick up their son after Little League practice. Her own mother had to be taken to a clinic twice a week. In between, there were housekeeping chores, meals to cook, and other responsibilities to discharge.

"It's just a rat race," she told Mark. "I run around with my tongue hanging out from morning till night. We have a nice home but I never get to enjoy it because I'm on the go all the time. Will life always be this hectic? I'm so discouraged!" She sank into a chair and stared into space.

Mark maneuvered her into his lap with her head on his shoulder. He stroked her hair and began to talk with her as one would a fretful child. He bragged on her versatility, her undergirding of the various members of the family, and he pointed out factors that indicated her schedule might ease off presently. Every now and then he punctuated his remarks with a kiss. No wonder Kathy recovered from her despondency and was up to shouldering her responsibilities again the next morning!

If there are family or social tensions, limited horizons, physical infirmities, material deficiencies, or other hindrances to a serene and satisfying life, a wife is going to have periods of depression. Husbands and others need to note symptoms of discouragement when they appear, and seek to counteract them.

Catherine Menninger, wife of the noted psychiatrist, tells of his unfailing custom of saying *thank you* for even the most trifling courtesies. She states, "In those two words, 'thank you,' he made me feel needed and appreciated. 'Thank you' is like a road sign that shows your mate he's going in the right direction."

The obligation to be a source of encouragement to one's mate is an implication of the marriage arrangement ordained by God. Paul says in Ephesians 5:33, ". . . let every one of you in particular so love his wife even as himself; and the wife see that she reverence [obey, praise, honor] her husband."

Following these instructions will lift the spirit of either spouse, because after all, each mate should be the best friend the other one has.

3
Children Can
Be Encouraged

Ronnie Clarke was not doing well in school, so his mother went to see Miss Bentley, his teacher, to discuss it with her.

"He seems to have difficulty concentrating, and is listless. He complains of a dry mouth. Do you think there is anything the matter physically?" the young woman asked.

"I don't know what it would be," Mrs. Clarke replied. "We all had our yearly checkups not long ago and he had an OK on everything. Now his sister had two or three little items that could be improved, yet she does superior work. Her report card is always good."

Grasping that as a clue, Miss Bentley said, "I wonder if he is suffering from depression. Do you hold up his sister as an example to him, and brag on her attainments to his discredit?"

"I never heard of a child his age suffering from depression," Mrs. Clarke replied, ignoring the question.

"He could be discouraged over his low level of attainment as compared to his sister's achievements. A child's attitude toward himself is formed within the home. The parents are usually responsible if he holds himself in low esteem and is discouraged by it. You know, children often feel and react to situations more sensitively than we realize. Maybe what Ronnie needs is encouragement. Try expressing appreciation for his good qualities—and make no mistake, he has a number of them. You might be surprised at how it would help him emerge from his depression and do better in his school work."

"I just never heard of a child suffering from depression," the mother repeated.

"Maybe not," the teacher acquiesced, "but little folks do have many elements to discourage them. You see, they have to start from scratch. Even though their physical development is sort of automatic with proper food, rest, and exercise, personality development is a big job. They have to learn to make choices and decisions. That's often hard, even for grown-ups. And we all know how discouraging a wrong choice can be."

"Yes, I remember Betty Lou elected to wear one of her better dresses on the day they were going to finger paint," Mrs. Clarke recalled. "I advised her not to, but she was determined so I let her. You can guess what happened. She came in the door looking as long-faced as a donkey."

Miss Bentley nodded and then pointed out, "They have to learn to get along with other people. They have to learn what attitudes or actions will cause them to be rejected, and which will bring acceptance. And they have to work at it on two levels, with their peers and with adults. Yes, decision making is discouraging for children. They have plenty of things to discourage them."

"I remember when I was in the fifth grade," Mrs. Clarke laughed. "A friend of my father's came to our room with an offer of a New Testament for each one who would promise to read it. I wanted to rate with Mr. Olson, who was a member of the Gideons, an organization held in high esteem by my father. But, due to some perverse notion, I didn't want to bind myself to reading the New Testament. I finally took it, but I was out of sorts inside myself for days. I remember Dad said I didn't seem very happy about receiving it."

Again Miss Bentley nodded, and then said, "Contradictory standards are another discouraging factor for young people. They are told they must be honest in all matters involving money, but they don't see it practiced by others. Once when I was teaching in another city, one of my pupils asked me, 'Miss Bently, what does it mean to *pad* an expense account?'

"Without thinking, I said, 'It means you tell the company you work for that you spent more money for meals or motel rooms or something like that than you actually did pay for them.' Too late I asked him, 'Why do you want to know?'

"He said, 'I heard Dad tell Mother he hoped to pad his expense account enough to get her a new sweater.' Then this youngster asked, 'Miss Bentley, if I told my folks my school lunch was ten cents a day more than it is, I could get enough money to go to a movie, couldn't I?'

"When I tried to explain why he shouldn't do it, he just walked away, but he was grumpy for several days. I don't know what you'd call it, but I'd call it depression due to disillusionment. Yes, kids this age can be discouraged by double standards and a lot more things."

Mrs. Clarke isn't the only one who has failed to recognize that children, as well as adults, can be discouraged. Despite the fact that young ones are supposed to be carefree and lighthearted, many of them think seriously and can be disheartened by life on their level.

Nita was such a one. She told her mother, "Patty and Judy wanted me to stop at their house to look at some pictures that Patty found in her brother's room. I asked them what they were pictures of and Judy giggled and said, 'Men and women in their birthday clothes.' I told them I had to come home and practice my music lesson."

Nita did go to the piano, but her heart didn't seem to be in her practicing. There were long pauses between scales. Her mother peeked in and noted that her daughter was just sitting at the piano staring into space.

"What's the matter, Nita?" she asked.

"Oh, Mother," the dispirited girl confided, "I just get tired of saying no."

Life is full of endless enticements to evil, and coping with them is discouraging business for younger persons, as well as older. Nita's mother had an opportunity to encourage her with words of appreciation for her resistance to temptation. All children need that encouragement.

An often-ignored way of encouraging children and young people, or in fact anyone, is by listening to them.

If we brush them off or even tell them we haven't time to listen just now, we discourage them. How would we feel if, when we prayed, God gave us the "busy signal," or conveyed the impression, *I don't have time to listen to you now.*

A mother noticed that her teenage son made frequent visits to a nearby young widow's home although there were no children there. She became concerned and questioned him about it.

"Why do you like to visit Mrs. Green?" she cross-examined him.

He hesitated, then answered, "She has time to listen to what happens at school, how the last ball game went, and things like that," he explained.

Another reason youth may become discouraged is over-exposure to the complications of life. Television, movies, newspapers, magazines, and books, as well as real life, are daily confronting them with life's problems and failures, as well as its possible successes and satisfactions. Before they reach adulthood, they recognize that the former often outnumber the latter. They need to be encouraged to believe that within their scope of attainment is the power to influence which it shall be.

Debbie, age fourteen, told her older sister, "I'll probably end up as an unwed mother just like that girl in the story."

"You can if you don't care," her sister told her, "but there's a better way open if you want to take it. Make up your mind what kind of life you'd like to have and then work at making yourself the kind of person who could achieve that kind of life.

"You've got a good start with a lot of things in your

favor," she went on. "You're nice looking, physically healthy, have a normal mind, an opportunity to get a good education, and a lot of us are rooting for you. Just don't muff the deal by sacrificing a future *best* for a present *desire*. Set your goals and don't be satisfied with anything less."

Children need encouragement, and it behooves older persons to take note of it. Decide now to strive to make every contact with a young person a positive experience for him. It will be a plus transaction for you as well.

4
Parents Can
Be Encouraged

Jean hung up the phone from her daily call to her parents. She had detected discouragement in her mother's voice as she said, "Your father's arthritis has flared up again. He's in a lot of pain."

Jean wondered what she could do to brighten the day for them. Her father wouldn't enjoy going anywhere in his condition, so that was out. She kept pondering the possibilities as she went about her household chores, talking to the Lord about the matter as she worked.

"I guess I'll just share myself," she finally concluded aloud. "Maybe if I go over and lunch with them, that will break up the day's monotony. I'll take a dish of tuna salad because Mom is so fond of that and—let's see—Dad likes those little bitty meatballs with spaghetti."

She took a package of hamburger from the deep-freeze, thankful she had already rolled it into tiny balls before freezing it. Then she went to the phone to notify her parents of her plans.

Children often overlook the fact that sharing of self is usually one of the most heartening things they can do for their parents. Grown sons and daughters get so involved with their segment of life that their parents are relegated to the background. Children often think they don't have time for their parents. Besides, they reason, their folks don't really *need* anything.

What a mistaken conclusion! They do have basic needs that are not being met. For instance, there is the matter of self-confidence. Because of their waning powers and reduced usefulness (as they see it), their self-esteem decreases or completely collapses. Carelessness or neglect on the part of their offspring or others is taken as evidence that they are not worth bothering about.

Harry's parents summered in a resort community within easy driving distance of his home, yet he rarely communicated or visited with them. It was a source of discouragement to the parents because their hometown friends assumed they all enjoyed considerable fellowship. Thoughtlessly they asked questions which embarrassed the parents because they were not kept abreast of their son's activities and did not know the answers.

Parents may also become discouraged because of their diminishing opportunities. Because of their age, reduced income, physical handicaps, or other limitations, there are fewer activities open to them. With our society being as youth-oriented as it is, there is a tendency to write parents off as has-beens who have nothing to contribute to society.

Mr. and Mrs. Purdue had been successful and

popular citizens of a smalltown community. But when he retired from business and she developed a heart condition, the demands for their presence at various functions lessened.

Soon Mary, their daughter, noticed that her mother was becoming less interested in keeping up her personal appearance. Formerly, her clothes had been of great importance to her. Meanwhile, Mary's father became obsessed with the fear that Social Security benefits would be cut down or eliminated by the government which would leave him and his wife without sufficient income. So both parents were in need of encouragement.

Mary began to look for ways to get them out among people. She took them to a dinner show where a sleight-of-hand artist performed. Upon hearing her father say there was nothing to it—that he, too, could accomplish such feats with a little practice—she took him at his word, bought him a magician's kit, and borrowed library books on the subject for him to study. He did prove adept at the art and before long was in demand as an amateur entertainer.

Meanwhile, Mary inveigled a Little Theater group to which she belonged into using her mother as the stylish widow in a play they were giving. This boosted the lady's ego and lifted her out of her depressed state, at least for the time being.

Churches, service clubs, and other organizations might do well to keep an inventory of the talents of various senior citizens, and search for ways to involve them in worthwhile activities. There might be fewer suicides, cases of senility and emotional breakdowns if this were practiced.

Loneliness is one of the frequent factors contributing to depression. This may be especially true in the case of those who have lost a mate. Joan and Luke seemed to be unusually alert to such situations, and one or both of them would work at lifting the bereaved one's spirits. They used phone calls, letters, and invitations to share an experience as means of helping such persons. They might ask the bereaved to come by their home to see their rock collection, or suggest that they go bowling together.

Monotony and boredom are other causes which contribute to depression. Most of what has been suggested to lift the spirits of the lonely would apply here as well.

Jack's mother was a semi-invalid. His father, who bore much of the responsibility of caring for her, was about as housebound as she was. Jack made it a habit to phone them on his lunch hour. He tried not to let his calls be dull and routine. He would joke, "Did you hear about the mailman who had gout in his big toe?" or sometimes he had an amusing incident to relate about one of the grandchildren. He always strove to talk on a positive plane and he never let his own moodiness leak through into his conversations. This daily gesture of thoughtfulness went a long way toward keeping his parents from becoming depressed. He felt the payphone tariff was well spent. He did not, however, fail to see them personally from time to time.

Eddie was a warmhearted retiree who went to his father-in-law's cottage nearly every day for ten o'clock coffee. After a few minutes of sociability, he returned to his own program. Maybe this daily custom was one reason the father-in-law rarely suffered from depression.

Worry and uncertainty about how their children will "turn out" often discourage parents. It may or may not be justified. It may or may not be due to their fear that failure on their part is a factor. Of course, the surest morale booster in that event is evidence in the life of their offspring that they are maturing creditably and successfully.

The Smiths' daughter had gone to a distant city to pursue her career. She did not write too frequently nor specifically about her life there. They were depressed about it until she sent a newspaper clipping reporting her selection as chairman of a civic committee. That cheered them and minimized their misgivings.

Too often, perhaps, sons and daughters take the attitude, "I'm of age. My life is my own to live as I please." On that basis, it may be legitimate to ignore the feelings of one's parents. But is it kind or compassionate?

When dwindling satisfaction from other sources dismay parents, isn't it a responsibility, an opportunity, even a challenge, for their offspring to be their spirit lifters?

Remember, it isn't so much the things you did for your parents as the things you *didn't* do that will haunt you after they've passed from the scene. If they are already gone, make amends for your omissions with them by doing for some other parents what you might have done for your own. Look around you for someone who needs a spirit lifter. Be one, *today!*

5
Kinsmen Can
Be Encouraged

Myrna told her neighbor, "Whenever I get the blues, I like to talk to my daughter-in-law. She always cheers me up."

"What did you say?" the neighbor asked in an incredulous voice. She couldn't believe she'd heard right.

"It's a fact," Myrna assured her. "Like this morning, my neuritis was bothering me so I thought I'd bake a cake to take my mind off it. I got it in the oven all right, but a friend got me on the phone and held me so long it burned to a crisp. Actually, she was pouring out her troubles and I forgot the cake while trying to help her.

"Then, when I went to take it out of the oven, I burned myself. That made me drop the pan and the cake popped out and broke all to pieces so I had a big cleanup job. I was ready to give up by the time I was through. I collapsed in a chair and called my daughter-in-law, to tell her my sad story."

"What did she say?" curiosity prompted the neighbor to ask.

"It wasn't so much *what* she said as the *way* she said it. She just sounded like she loved me and was sorry I'd had a bad time. She even asked me if I wanted her to come over and clean up the mess, but I had already done that. Of course I wouldn't have let her anyway, but she's the sweetest thing."

"She must be. It always makes me depressed to think of my son getting married, as he eventually will, because I'm scared my daughter-in-law might not like me."

"Just ask God to give you love for her. Note her good points and appreciate them. And let her know you do. Kinsfolk ought to appreciate and encourage each other. Life would be a lot pleasanter if they would," Myrna ended the conversation.

Aunts, uncles, nieces, nephews, grandparents, and in-laws all suffer from discouragements, just as anyone else does. Instead of thinking critically about a kinsman's difficulties, and concluding that he brought the trouble on himself, we ought to be the first to seek to encourage him.

Basically, to help one member of a family is to contribute directly or indirectly to the welfare of all. For, if a member's depression becomes public knowledge, some of the relatives will very possibly be blamed for it or be discredited by it, particularly if it becomes acute. Furthermore, it can start a chain reaction which may detract from the serenity of many.

Willa was depressed because her husband was an alcoholic, which seems a justifiable reaction. But because of her habitual gloominess, their teenage children found home an unpleasant place to be. They spent as little time there as possible. This added to

Willa's unhappiness, but she failed to do anything about it.

People began to talk about the children running loose, and some of these comments reached the ears of Willa's brother's wife. She was embarrassed by them and told her husband she was disheartened by such talk. She told him he ought to do something about his brother's family.

Actually, who should have tried to inspirit whom? Did not each one have a responsibility to try to encourage the other? The mother her teeners, and the teeners their mother? The man his brother, and his wife the sister-in-law? And wouldn't it have contributed to the best interests of all if they had? Too many times our kinsfolk's difficulties arouse contempt instead of compassion and, thereby, we generate discouragement rather than encouragement.

Perhaps with kinsmen more than with any other persons, encouragement should be a constant attitude, a way of life. It should be the fragrance of Christ involuntarily wafted to those to whom we are related, more than a deliberate speech or act,that will have impact on them. Through our daily manner of coping with life we could become to them a haven of comfort when they are in distress. They should feel assured of our concern and sympathy when clouds arise on their horizon.

"Blessed be God, even the Father of our Lord Jesus Christ, the Father of mercies, and the God of all comfort; Who comforteth us in all our tribulation, that we may be able to comfort them which are in any trouble, by the comfort wherewith we ourselves are comforted of God" (II Corinthians 1:3,4).

As this passage tells us, God has mediated encouragement to us in order that we may in turn convey it to others. Are we doing so, especially to those who are our kinsfolk?

Wayne Pierce recounts a story in *Home Life* magazine of a three-year-old child's encouragement to his parents on the occasion of the accidental death of his maternal grandfather. He unconsciously bolstered them by his sweet way of accepting the tragedy. If a three-year-old child can spontaneously communicate encouragement to his parents, shouldn't we be available for a similar ministry to any of our kinsfolk who may need it?

6
Co-workers Can
Be Encouraged

Noel Cox was the head of a big corporation. He had a plush office with vice-presidents, secretaries, office boy, and a host of others at his beck and call. Ordinarily he functioned with aplomb, wearing his authority easily, yet with a firmness that required efficient performances of his wishes. But for two or three days he had not been himself. Marie, his personal secretary, and Bob, the office boy, had noticed it. Being kin in Christ, they discussed it guardedly between themselves.

"He took only one bite out of that sandwich he sent out for," Bob commented. "Maybe he has ulcers or something else eating on him."

"He carries so much responsibility. He has to make weighty decisions," Marie contributed.

"And I suppose being top dog could be lonely," Bob offered. "You know, he might not dare drop his dignity and pal with some of the lesser lights. Something's sure making him glum."

"He gets all the criticism, too," Marie remarked. "No matter what goes wrong, all the rest can pass the buck until it ends with him."

"I'm glad I'm not in his shoes, but what can *we* do to cheer him up?"

"We can pray for him. You find a place to get to yourself and talk to the Lord about him. I'll go to the supply closet," Marie said, as if it had been her resort on other occasions.

No matter what may be the vocational area of our lives—medical, legal, business, sales, military, civil service, political, or any other—there are co-workers around us who need their spirits lifted. In places of employment, people often have fellow employees under them, as well as over them who need encouragement.

Stan was in the delicate position of having one co-worker under him and another above him who did not get along well together. Relations between them were strained and Jud, the one below Stan, was very discouraged about it. Although he had a wife and two children to support, he indicated more than once that he was of "a mind to just quit" and return to his home state, even though it would mean sacrificing a good future and having a lower income.

Stan and Jud rode to work together, so Stan took advantage of that period to encourage his co-worker to "tough it out" until such time as he or the boss might be transferred to another post of duty. With Stan's friendly support and wise counsel, Jud concluded that staying would be a good thing to do. In time, Jud was transferred and received a promotion because someone offered him encouragement at a time when discouragement might have ruined his career.

Then there was Howard who held a supervisory position in a bank. He was alert to all the employees' needs and problems. One day it might be one of the telephone operators who seemed disconsolate; another day someone else. For example, Ruthie, one of the tellers who was customarily bright and efficient, seemed heavy-spirited.

"How's your little one these days?" her overseer found opportunity to inquire.

"All right, I hope," Ruthie responded. "But I had to get a new baby-sitter while the regular one has a baby of her own. I'm not sure how they'll get along together. This is their first day."

"Would you like to step into my office and call home to find out?" Howard suggested. "I'll stand in for you here."

Ruthie came back with a shining face. "They're getting along fine. Thank you so much."

Another day it was John, an office machine mechanic who came periodically to check on various pieces of equipment. Howard noted that he wasn't as genial as usual, and had a grim look on his face as he performed his services. Howard called the man into his office on the pretext of asking about a typewriter.

"How's life treating you, John?" he inquired.

"Kind of rough," was the reply. "My wife is in the hospital. She had surgery."

"Is she doing all right?"

"As well as can be expected," John mimicked a female voice. "That's what they told me the day before my mother died, so it doesn't give me much peace of mind."

"John, the hospital's statement is a safe, conservative one to make. Call your doctor if you want additional assurance about her condition. But let me remind you that there is One who can give you peace of mind in any and all circumstances. Jesus Christ reminds us in John 14:27, 'Peace I leave with you, my peace I give unto you: not as the world giveth, give I unto you. Let not your heart be troubled, neither let it be afraid.' John, I'll be praying for your wife and you. I know God will work something good out of this."

"Thank you, sir," John said, "you make me feel better."

Sometimes the co-worker is neither below nor above one, but is the person at the bench or counter beside him.

Ann and Jane had both received notices terminating their employment the following week: "The management regrets that due to economic conditions they are compelled to . . ."

"We might have known it was coming, " Ann said. "With business as poor as it is, and neither one of us doing anything except standing around waiting for the customers who never come in.

"But I don't know what I'll do. Getting another job won't be easy, especially at my age.

"God knows all about it and will open a way. I have a little savings, but I hope I won't have to dig into it. There'll be our unemployment insurance for awhile."

"But what about when that runs out?"

"God will direct me as to what to do. He will provide."

"You really believe that, don't you?"

"Why shouldn't I? God is a gentleman and a

gentleman always keeps his promises. He won't let anything happen to me that does not have some kind of a blessing in it for me."

"I wish I could buy that kind of belief. It really holds you up, doesn't it?"

"But, Jane, you *can* have it. God offers you the same security if you'll only turn to Him and trust Him. He's so wonderful. He never fails. Don't cheat yourself. Let Him come in and fill that empty place in your heart."

"Just talking about it helps me to hope," Jane commented.

"He can give you a permanent lift, Jane, if you'll just take it on His terms."

It is not only co-workers in commercial enterprises who may need encouragement. Often those in volunteer organizations do, too.

Carol had been canvassing a block for the United Funds Campaign. As she was on the way to headquarters to turn in her report she encountered Laurie, who had been out on the same errand.

"Hi!" Carol greeted her. "How'd you get along?"

"Terrible! Five residents weren't at home. At least they didn't answer the door. Then there was one elderly woman that I'm sure didn't have anything to spare. The other two were plain nasty. One of them flatly refused to give, and the other one acted like she was being blackmailed. I'm embarrassed to take my cards in."

"Why don't you wait and try again with the ones who weren't home?" Carol suggested. "Maybe you could catch them there in the evening."

"I don't like to go out at night by myself," Laurie admitted. "I guess I'm scared of being mugged."

"Tell you what," Carol offered, "I'll go with you.

We'll give them a chance to finish their evening meal without being interrupted, but we won't wait too long, so we can catch them before they go out for the evening."

"Oh, Carol! Would you? That would be wonderful "

"I'll give you a ring and we'll meet at the same place we did awhile ago. I bet you'll have a good report to turn in after all," Carol told her.

D. L. Moody is quoted as saying, "I have never known God to use a discouraged person." Volunteer church workers, more than any others, are apt to suffer setbacks that discourage them; therefore, they above all people, should be strengthened by their fellow Christians.

Abbie was a worker in the nursery department of the church. Little recognition was given for her faithful service. One Sunday morning she developed a headache, and the children seemed especially fretful. Something went wrong with the public address system so that she couldn't hear the music and the pastor's sermon. Dispirited by the combination of factors, she made up her mind to resign.

She was caused to alter her decision by what one of the Sunday School teachers said when she came for her baby. She remarked, "I can always forget about Doug when I teach the lesson, and then relax while I concentrate on the pastor's sermon, because I know Doug is in the competent hands of someone who cares."

Back in Isaiah's time, we are told, "They helped every one his neighbour; and every one said to his brother, Be of good courage" (Isaiah 41:6).

Why don't we do more of that *today?*

7
Fellow Citizens Can
Be Encouraged

A business matter took Les to the office of his insurance agent. The latter was back on the job with limitations after a fair recovery from a heart attack. It was obvious that the relaxed attitude toward life which he had formerly, was gone. He seemed tense and rather depressed, which of course was not surprising. It was a challenge to Les to try to lift his spirits.

"It's good to see you back on the job," he told him.

"I don't know how much good I'll be," was the pessimistic response.

"Plenty," Les assured him. "What you have in your head is what helps us businessmen, and a faulty ticker isn't going to change that."

"But I can't plan ahead anymore. I don't know whether I'll be here or in the hospital again . . . ."

"Well, do we ever really know what the future holds for us? If you'll think it through, you'll realize you don't know; you only take it for granted. You never really know whether or not a car might jump the curb and plow right through here, or whether an explosion at the service station might level the building. The Bible says our times are in *His* hands (Psalms 31:15). It also says 'the steps of a good man are ordered by the Lord'" (Psalms 37:23).

Then he went on, "All we need to do is place ourselves in His hands and live one day at a time, or even an hour, or a moment, trusting Him with all of our uncertainties."

"I guess you have something there. I'll give it some thought," the agent promised. It seemed to Les that his face looked a little less strained as he added, "Now what can I do for you?"

Because a majority of one's fellow citizens leave God out of their lives, many of the assurances that might be offered them fall on indifferent ears and produce no reactions. They sometimes are met with argument about the wisdom or goodness of a God who would permit the circumstances which are responsible for their discouragement. In view of these possibilities, one of the most potent factors in cheering them up may be the buoyant life pattern of the one who consistently lives above depression.

The whole community knew about the rough times which had beset Henry. His wife had been killed when, through no fault of their own, they had collided with a drunken driver. Henry's leg had been broken in a manner that left him with a limp. He was trying to rear his motherless boys to be solid citizens. His misfortunes had resulted in a slump in his business. It was requiring hard work to build it back to a paying proposition. His parents, residents of a nearby community, were known to be dissolute and of no help to him.

"Did you ever hear Henry complain?" someone asked at a Rotary Club meeting. No one present could recall that he had.

"He's always cheerful and looking for matters to get better," one member volunteered.

"I remember talking to him the week after his wife was buried," said one. "Even then, he could smile and say God was good that the boys hadn't been in the car and were spared."

"And when that city slicker's lawyer beat him out of the just settlement he had coming, it never made him bitter," another chimed in.

"He makes me ashamed of myself for every getting the blues," another admitted. "He's always on the upbeat."

"Did you ever tell him he's an inspiration to you?" a member queried.

"We ought to do something to let him know we esteem him," someone suggested.

That points up another phase of spirit lifting which will be discussed more fully in a later chapter. *Words of encouragement can often be reinforced with actions.*

A couple went by a hospital to pick up the wife of a patient and take her to dinner. While their order was being served, they were able to recall many of God's promises. They helped her get a new perspective on events.

"You'll never know how that lifted me and gave me courage to continue my long vigil," she told them later.

Sometimes an acquaintance betrays that he is suffering from depression due to a sense of guilt or remorse. In such a situation, we may help him to emerge from his gloominess by reminding him of God's readiness to forgive and forget our shortcomings and transgressions. Many Scripture passages (especially Isaiah 38:17 and 43:25) could be cited to help relieve his sorrow.

A fellow citizen is often encouraged just by learning that someone is aware that he is in a discouraging situation, and interested in helping him through it.

"We're concerned along with you for your little girl in the hospital," could be the salutation at the post office. Or, "I hope your business is picking up," could be the greeting at the bank.

"Is your father making a satisfactory recovery from his operation?" could be the query at the PTA meeting.

In his article, "The Healing Touch of Attention," D. C. Smith points out, "Attention heals. The golden coin of attention . . . learn to pay it graciously and gladly, and the dividends will come pouring back to you."

Listening is a form of attention which gives encouragement. This was demonstrated in the case of two acquaintances. Not only was Ruby talkative; her words were often caustic. She seemed to purposely demean Bonnie, often hurting her friend's feelings. For the sake of a vocational relationship between their husbands, Bonnie endured Ruby's patronizing ways and frequent disparagements, and accepted the role of listener.

After their husbands' joint tenure on a government job terminated, and the two couples went their separate ways, Ruby and her husband came to visit Bonnie and her husband. Again Ruby monopolized the conversation. Upon her departure, however, she paid this tribute to her hostess: "I've especially enjoyed talking to you. I've always thought of you as my *listening* friend, Bonnie, because you always took time to listen to my every problem."

Of course, the effectiveness of encouragements, even the quickie kind in greetings, depends on the sincerity and actual concern of the one who offers them. If we would be as interested in the needs and problems of our neighbors as we are about the gossip items we hear in respect to them, we might do a lot to alter the pattern of their lives.

"Love thy neighbor as thyself," is too often a bit of rhetoric, instead of a daily obligation to be alert and eager to brighten the days of others.

8
Strangers Can Be Encouraged

As she stuffed soiled clothes into the machine at the Laundromat, Linda glanced at the woman operating the next washer. She believed she remembered seeing her the previous week, and she had been impressed then, as now, with the forlorn look on the girl's face.

I wonder what personal problem she has that makes her look that way, Linda thought to herself. She tried to catalog possible causes: ill health, a backache or other pain. Did her hands look a bit crippled with something like arthritis? But wasn't she too young for that?

Or could it be a heartache? Maybe she had an alcoholic husband, or somebody in the hospital. Linda's vivid imagination could picture a parent with terminal cancer. Or maybe she had a problem: Is it wrong to go to bingo parties? Or, is it all right to buy a new dress when your husband will be laid off next week? *Life presents so many difficulties, it's no wonder a person looks discouraged,* she concluded.

But what can I do about it? was her next thought. Silently she breathed a prayer for guidance before smiling at her neighbor and remarking, "We washed them last week, but our linens are dirty and need to be done over again. It's a never ending job, isn't it?"

The girl's tense face relaxed ever so little as she nodded an assent.

"I guess we should be thankful we can come here instead of having to rub them on a rock in the river like I saw some foreign women doing on television awhile back," Linda suggested.

"I sure couldn't do that," the girl commented.

Emboldened, Linda asked, "Do you watch television much? What is your favorite program?"

Adroitly she went on to forge links of friendliness by bits of conversation. Maybe, with the Lord's help, she could do something about the expression of discouragement she had noted on the woman's face. At least she could try while the washer churned and spun.

Often those who are strangers do need encouragement. Frequently they can be more readily cheered by someone who doesn't know them than by one who does. Several possibilities could account for this. Perhaps their near ones are so absorbed with their own worries that they give no thought to the other's needs. They might not even have been aware of the person's state of gloominess.

Or perhaps the person has a chronic case of blues and near ones have given up trying to lift his spirits. Or they might not have known how to go about it. Maybe the friends have few resources on which to draw for encouragement for themselves, let alone another.

Or one's downheartedness may seem so justifiable that friends think it fitting to merely groan with him instead of trying to cheer him. That was not Jesus' way. Many times He is quoted as saying, "Be of good cheer." His greetings and admonitions were upbeat notes.

On the other hand, the stranger who needs encouragement may not merely be a person to whom one has not been introduced. He may actually be a newcomer to the community, and his depression may be related to this.

Gretchen's husband had received a job transfer which brought them to a new community. He met people and made new friends at his place of employment, but Gretchen did not have that advantage. She was, therefore, very pleased when the friendly lady in the next apartment invited her to a coffee one morning. There she not only became acquainted with a couple of other apartment residents, but also some other young women. One of them invited her to accompany her to a tea at her church the next day. There she met still other women and soon became happy and busy in the church's program.

Perhaps the stranger is lonely because he is acutely homesick for persons and places he has left behind. Along with this may be unfamiliarity with the places, people, and customs of his present residence. And he or she may have a fear of not being accepted in the new location, of never feeling as if he belongs or is at home.

An American was so journing in Germany. Undertaking to go shopping one day, she became confused about the direction she should take. Disheartened over her predicament, she timidly accosted a young German girl and named the street she needed to reach. The girl could not speak English any more fluently than the American could speak German. She recognized the name of the street, but could not explain the route to it.

Motioning the inquirer to follow her, she walked several blocks to escort the stranger to the desired street. Then she returned the same way she had come, evidently having gone out of her way to assist the foreigner. The visitor wondered how many Americans would have gone to the same trouble to accommodate a visitor in their country. It was an encouraging incident.

During past wars, many servicemen brought home Oriental or Asian brides. These women represent a special need for encouragement and help. Encouragement may begin with a smile or gesture, a friendly attitude toward them. In some instances, encouragement has continued in the form of English lessons and other loving ministries offered in the spirit of Christ. It sometimes results in their being transformed into Christian personalities.

There was the case of a Korean war bride who was a Buddhist, but had a Christian grandmother. The girl spoke broken but understandable English. She had perhaps been helped by programs she watched over an educational television station. There was a Good News Club in the trailer park where she lived which her four-year-old daughter attended.

Adults visiting the parents of its Club members were the first people to knock on her door in the two years she had lived there. The Korean girl hid. The church followed up with additional visitation and the head of the family came to church. Because the wife had not permitted visitors from the church to enter the home, an appointment was made through the husband for them to call. This time they were admitted. Several visits followed. She was invited to meetings and finally she came with her husband to church.

She was desperately lonely. She never left the trailer, not even to go to the grocery store. She felt she was stuck (she later explained) with her husband, their two children, and her pregnancy with a third. As she was given attention by members of the church, she began to bloom before their eyes. She needed their encouragement and they were generous with their time.

Eventually, she went forward in church, motivated by a desire to be an accepted part of it. In a personal interview, her pastor explained the need to become a Christian before joining a church. She could not read and her understanding was limited, but when she prayed to receive Christ, it was evident that the Holy Spirit had changed her heart. Subsequently, she was able to explain how desperately she had needed encouragement at that point in her life, and how God had met her needs through some of His children.

In *The War Cry*, the following story was related: In a bus station a woman was sitting beside a Mexican woman when she noticed that huge tears were rolling down the woman's cheeks. When addressed kindly in Spanish, the little lady poured out a sorrowful tale.

Her husband had died suddenly in the great city. Notified by authorities, the woman had used all the money she had for a bus ticket. Since she had no money for mortician's fees or burial, the body would be given to a medical school. Brokenhearted, she was about to return home with her preschool child.

Missing her own bus, her benefactor took her to the

Salvation Army where arrangements were made for her care and lodging, and for holding the body pending efforts on her behalf. Her deceased American husband was found to have had a son by a previous marriage who came and made funeral arrangements and also took his stepmother back to her home.

How much this stranger owed to the encouragement afforded her by one of God's children! The oft-quoted declaration of Christ, ". . . [when] ye have done it unto the least of these my brethren, ye have done it unto me" (Matthew 25:40), is sufficient motive for anyone to seek to lift the spirit of a stranger.

9
People Need Encouragement About Their Appearance

Several television commercials picture a man looking at himself in the mirror and being shocked and dismayed by what he sees there. It may be gray hair, an overnight growth of whiskers, or dingy teeth. Of course, in the advertising world such discouraging factors can always be overcome by use of the right product, but in real life there are often items of appearance that are less easily corrected.

A person may be downhearted because of his wardrobe. He may consider it inadequate, out of date, or for some other reason, unsuitable.

A woman of limited means found herself having to wear the same dress repeatedly. Her discomfort about it was relieved when a friend commented, "Elsie, I'm always glad to see you in that dress. It makes you look so trim and neat."

Sometimes people err in their choice of what to wear on a given occasion. A man may arrive at an event in an open-collared sports shirt, only to find all the rest of the men in ties. Or perhaps a woman comes in a street dress and the other women are in floor-length frocks. Unless someone does something to offset their embarrassment, the occasion may become a nightmare for them.

One can help set them at ease by friendliness and conversation. If they bring up the subject of their appearance one may assure them that their presence is valued in any costume. (Ask God to enable you to value it.) Assure them that what they *are* is more important than what they *wear*. It may be an opportunity to witness by citing a Scripture, such as "Man looketh on the outward appearance, but the Lord looketh on the heart [at a man's thoughts]" (I Samuel 16:7b).

A sincere compliment is often effective in putting one at ease about his apparel. One can nearly always find something nice to say without being dishonest or hypocritical. For instance, a dress, despite a bulging fit, may be made of beautiful material. Well-chosen accessories may be commendable though the costume is not. Regardless of what is above them, a man's shoes may look comfortable. A shirt from material of an unattractive design may have colors that harmonize well with the slacks being worn.

Hair can be commended because of its color, styling, cleanness, luster, or luxurious growth. Eyes may be complimented for their size, color, emotional expression, such as tenderness, good will, sparkle, or humor. The teeth, lips, or even ears may be items to compliment.

A person may need to be encouraged to improve his appearance. Great delicacy and tact is required in such a situation. That person may, however, have resigned himself to the conclusion that nothing can be done to improve his appearance when such is not totally true.

Often people are dismayed by real or fancied disfigurements, such as an oversize nose. Usually it is best to ignore such defects if they actually do exist. But if the person himself refers to the drawback, then it is in order to try to encourage him. One can truthfully say, "Practically everyone has a blemish of some kind. I wouldn't worry about it if I were you." People can be reminded that God can use them in spite of their abnormalities.

A Christian woman sometimes gave way to discouragement because she considered herself homely and unattractive. Then she was challenged to pray, "Lord, help me to radiate Your light so dazzlingly that people can't see the chandelier."

A man who had a very obvious birthmark on his face was self-conscious about it. Rather than face the gaze of others, which he imagined was riveted on the vivid, red splotch, he kept in the background. Then he met Jesus Christ and became so excited about it that he had to share his Saviour with others, which he did with enthusiasm.

One such person became infected with it, too, and as a consequence committed his life to Christ. Back in his home town he was reporting the matter to a friend, who suspected he knew the one who had done the witnessing.

"Did he have a birthmark over a large area of his face?" the man asked.

The narrator looked confused, then said, "Blessed if I know. All I recall was his blue eyes that pierced through you to your very soul, and his voice, vibrant with love and urgency."

Some birth defects can be covered by cosmetics. Some irregularities can be minimized by the skilful use of makeup. Cleanliness improves any portion of the body. A change of diet might improve some people's appearance, as well as their health.

A little encouragement, given in the right manner, might be the stimulus to start some dispirited person on an improvement program that will enhance even his personality. The fact that a friend is interested, and the hope that a better appearance can be achieved may combine to lift someone's spirits.

Sally and Barb were eating their school lunches together. Sally paused, her sandwich halfway to her mouth.

"Barb!" she exclaimed, "you know what? You could style your hair like Greta Grayson [a current television star] and it would do wonders for you!"

"Come on, now, you know I couldn't look cute like she does."

"Wanna bet? Of course you'd have to begin with a good shampoo, one that made your hair squeaky clean."

"I've got some of that stuff they advertise that will make your hair like silk," Barb said.

"Fine! Bring it tomorrow and we'll go by my house after school and try it," Sally proposed.

"Don't expect too much," Barb cautioned, but there was a brighter, more hopeful expression on her face as she and her friend parted to go to their classes.

Because the impression one makes is directly related to his physical appearance, nearly all of us are sensitive about it. If we have a real or fancied deficiency, it is a point of vulnerability which makes us liable to discouragement. Therefore, one's appearance is a wide-open field for ministering encouragement to one's fellowman.

10
People Need Encouragement About Their Performances and Achievements

Out of the corner of his eye, Billy watched a neighbor cutting his grass. They were riding the same make and model of mower, but Billy's mom had said Mr. Blake did a better job than Billy did. Billy was trying to compare their respective yards. His mother was probably right, he dolefully concluded.

Mr. Blake stopped as his mower ran out of gas. He waved to Billy and yelled, "Nice work, Bill. You have a harder lawn to mow than I do because of the bumps and those shrubs you have to get around."

"Thank you, sir," Billy brightened. "I wish I could make our yard look as nice as yours."

"A little more practice and you'll have it looking better than mine," Mr. Blake assured him.

Regardless of what a person is doing, whether at home or in his place of employment, whether pursuing a hobby or grading a road, there are degrees of skill and efficiency with which the act is performed. Consequently, there are times when each of us wonders how we are doing. Often we end up discouraged because we are not doing better.

This is evidence that one's performance is an area where encouragement is needed and can be offered. Here again sincerity and honesty are called for, but there are many angles that can be applauded without resorting to flattery or exaggeration. For instance, one can commend the method—hand made, machine tooled—that is being used, even if the results are not all that might be desired.

When Harry went to make a parcel delivery, he found the elderly addressee preparing leaders for a fishing trip. He measured off a length of monofilament line, securely tied a hook to it, took a couple of split shot and, with pliers, attached them to the line. He then wound the leader around a bit of cardboard and fastened it there with a rubber band in readiness for use when required.

"You sure do a good job of that," Harry told the senior citizen. "I bet you catch a lot of fish."

Later, when by coincidence they met on the banks of a trout stream, the younger man called to his companion, "You ought to see this man make his leaders. He really does a professional job of it."

That bit of praise brought a smile to the older man's face and eased a mite the disappointment of the fish not biting.

The manner in which a job is done—carefully, neatly, precisely, thoroughly, enthusiastically, economically, speedily, quietly, artistically, skillfully—may be commended.

A woman was watching a friend knit. She commented, "I don't remember ever seeing anyone throw the yarn over the needle just the way you do. It makes it look really easy. Maybe I could learn to do it that way."

As in the case of Billy and his lawn mowing, one can comment on expected improvement or one can encourage about probable outcomes, such as an anticipated convenience or future enjoyments. A positive comment can raise the spirit, whereas a negative one may lower it.

One may observe another's haphazard way of setting out plants, but he need not say, "You'll never get any flowers the way you're planting those petunias." Rather, he can say, "My! It will brighten up that corner if you get a good yield of blooms on those plants."

A woman who visited her cousin found her preparing green beans for the freezer. She began helping her cousin stem and cut them. Privately she thought to herself, *These beans are too old and too wilted to make a very appetizing product.* Aloud she said, "It surely is handy to have food you can lift out of the freezer and use when you need something."

If we can't encourage another by what we say, we would do better to refrain from commenting. Look for what is right, not wrong, and talk about that.

Another area where people may be encouraged is in regard to their achievements.

"I used to hope and expect to make my mark in the world," a senior citizen with the name of Dudley recalled, "but I never made a name, won fame, or accumulated wealth," he said with a negative shake of his gray head.

"Wait a minute," his listener challenged, "I know two names you made. One is Wayne Dudley, mayor of Centertown, and the other is Harve Dudley, teacher in the high school. I call rearing two solid citizens such as they are a real achievement."

The words brought a glow of joy to the older man's face. "They *are* fine fellows, aren't they?" he said with pardonable pride.

Often when people become downcast, their spirits can be lifted by recognition of some personal achievement. It may be in any of several realms: vocation or career, craftsmanship, hobbies, human relations, community service, citizenship, sports.

The feeling that one has no achievements to his credit in *any* area is most discouraging. Of course, that is not apt to be true. Probably everyone is proficient or excels in some area of life. Something he has done is noteworthy in some respect. One way of recalling it for encouragement's sake is to inquire, "What was the most satisfying thing you ever did?"

Queried thus, one disconsolate woman after a moment of thought laughed in an embarrassed manner and then reported, "I guess it was when I won a blue ribbon for a pie I baked."

"Tell me about it," her questioner urged. The woman's face lit up as she talked and by the time the two parted she was in good spirits.

For some, achievement will be in the present rather than the past tense. Aboard a jet liner, Larry's seatmate was a grim-faced fellow who stared straight ahead as if in another world. Larry sought to start a conversation with him without much success until he said, "I see you have a Fletcher Foundation emblem in your lapel. That must be interesting work."

That stimulated the man to talk. Before he realized it, he had launched into an enthusiastic account of the

Foundation's program and accomplishments. His face actually had a glow on it when the conversation terminated because of their arrival at their destination. As they parted, the man explained: "I came here to attend the funeral of a dear friend. Naturally I was depressed. Talking with you made the time pass quickly and raised my spirits."

Larry fingered the book in his pocket he had hoped to read while on the plane, but he had abandoned the idea when he noted that his seatmate seemed to need his spirits lifted. Now he gave thanks that he had sensed the Spirit's leading.

Sometimes one can encourage a fellowman by recalling his past achievements. Paula's husband had to give up many of his activities because of an infirmity. This inactivity was discouraging to him.

Paula developed the knack of appreciating his past performances. Sometimes on wash days she would say, "I always give thanks for the way you fixed my clothesline on a pulley. It saves me so many steps." Or, "That was a help when you put the new knob on the teakettle for me. The old one wobbled so." Or, "I've often appreciated your putting that extra light in the basement. It makes it so much easier for me to find what I'm looking for." She noticed that such comments seemed to cheer her husband, at least temporarily.

Conversely, one can sometimes inspirit and challenge another by appreciating what he is *going* to do. Mac told his wife, "The girls will look nice in their new dresses when you get them made." Another time he said, "I'm looking forward to that new dessert you said you were going to try. I know it will be fantastic." Because his wife lacked self-confidence, such comments were encouraging to her.

Len had served unobtrusively for years in his church as interpreter for the deaf. One Sunday morning, without warning, the pastor called on him for the benediction. Len was obviously startled and at a loss for words.

After church, in an effort to relieve embarrassment, the pastor planned to call Len and offer to give fair warning in the future. But before he could reach the phone, it rang. The voice was Len's. "I'm sorry I was so startled this morning. You see, I've been a member of this church for seventeen years, and today is the first time anyone has ever asked me to pray publicly. Pastor, if you'll call on me again in a few weeks, I promise I'll be prepared."

"I know you will," the pastor assured him. From then on, the pastor did call on Len from time to time. It encouraged the man and he grew spiritually and increased in usefulness to his church and to his Lord.

It should be kept in mind that one need not have achieved the ultimate before his attainments can be recognized. There are different levels of participation and success. This should especially be borne in mind with children.

Benny was learning to fish but wasn't having much success and that disgruntled him. His father cheered him with the comment, "You're doing a good job of casting. Being able to flip your lure where you want it to land will help you get fish at some future time, if not today. Keep at it."

When the woman who anointed Jesus at the house of Simon, the leper, was being criticized for her act, Jesus praised her performance with the words, "She hath done what she could . . ." (Mark 14:8). What an example Jesus set!

Anyone who has performed to the limit of his ability —what he or she could—is to be encouraged. Unfortunately, most of us fall short of that. We don't measure up to our *coulds*. By all means, let us encourage those who do.

11
People Need
Encouragement
About Their
Failures

In today's world, all kinds and degrees of failure may be encountered. Frequently, there is the parent who seems to have failed in rearing his child to responsible citizenship. Nearly as numerous may be vocational failures, those who have not succeeded in a business venture, or who have lost their job. Along with the latter is the one who, though he retains a job, cannot earn sufficient income for his family's requirements.

Additionally there are those who, though gainfully employed, feel or realize that they are not making a worthwhile contribution to society. Also, there are those who are failing in marriage or other human relations. So, failure may involve anything from spoiling a batch of jelly to being divorced or going bankrupt.

It is easy to look at some segment of a fellowman's life and see that he has failed. It may even be very evident why he has failed. One might have a strong impulse to point it out to him with a few well-chosen words. But wait a minute — will that help him or will it discourage him?

Barnabas, (so nicknamed, it is said, because it means *encourager*) earned the name through helping "failures." He jeopardized or maybe forfeited his own material security by selling his land and giving the receipts to the apostles for distribution to the needy— persons who probably were thought of as financial failures.

Next he helped Paul, who had failed to convince the early disciples that he had become a bona fide follower of Jesus Christ. Later, Barnabas bolstered the spirits of John Mark who had "washed out" on a missionary journey with Paul. Paul had counted John Mark as a failure because he had left them and gone home from a mission on which the three had embarked.

Barnabas evidently realized, as all of us need to do, that though the cause of failure may not necessarily be justified, it can be understood if one has love. Failure calls for compassion, not criticism. It presents an opportunity to up-spirit one who is probably down-hearted enough without additional discouragements from others.

There are many reasonable causes for failures. First, failure may be due to circumstances beyond one's control. This is frequently, though by no means invariably, the cause of business failures. Earl had been making a satisfactory income through manufacture of an item employed in processing a certain kind of fish. The species became contaminated at its source and further canning of it was banned. Earl's business was ruined and he became a "financial failure" through no fault of his own. Yet people who did not take the trouble to understand the facts downgraded him, thus adding to his discouragement. He was about to conclude that he was a failure when a Christian businessman gave him the lift which reversed his circumstances.

Failure is often due to background deficiencies. A person fails because his early environment and training did not equip him or her to cope with the types of problems which arise in modern living. Brenda was such a one. Reared in a small, sleepy community, she met a fellow from a nearby air base. He was intrigued by her naivete. It made him feel so wise. Besides, she was pretty, witty, and winsome. He quickly proposed.

All went well until he was discharged from the service and they returned to a setting of luxury and sophistication. Brenda encountered customs and situations entirely foreign to her. She failed under the pressures and soon found herself a divorcee. Because of her inexperience, she did not even get a good financial settlement.

Penniless and too proud to go home, she tried suicide. The Salvation Army became her helper and, by their concern and ministry, inspirited her with courage to start a new life. They convinced her she was a person of worth created in the image of God and, as such, had potentialities for usefulness.

Failure may be due to unfortunate personality traits. Sometimes the one who fails because of them is not aware of his flaws, or he may not consider them critical factors in his life. Or he may be painfully aware of them, but unsuccessful in remedying them. Either the knowledge of his flaws or his inability to correct them may send him into a tailspin of dejection. Who is to minister to him, and how?

In Guy's case, it was a sympathetic college teacher who had witnessed some of his mistakes, and had heard of others. Returning to the classroom for a forgotten item, she found him still in his seat, staring morosely into space.

"Guy!" she hailed him. "What's the matter? You look as if you'd lost your last friend."

"I have," he agreed. "I'm a failure. I'll never get anywhere. I'm always talking when I should be listening. Every time I open my mouth, I put my foot in it. I just told Cindy she looked like she'd been siphoned off the top of a vinegar barrel. It made her hopping mad, but it was so. She looked as if she didn't have a friend in the world."

"It may have been true, but was it necessary or kind to say so? And wouldn't it have been fine if you could have cheered her up instead of downgrading her? Think what a difference it might have made in her day or even her life."

"I know. I never think of those things beforehand. I always blurt them out and am sorry afterward. I tell you, I'm a failure."

"Listen, Guy, self-pity won't help you, but God can. Have you talked to God about this shortcoming? You know the Psalmist prayed, 'Set a watch, O Lord, before my mouth' [Psalms 141:3]. Why don't you make that your prayer as you start the day? Also why don't you begin watching for opportunities to say something that will encourage instead of discourage people? Pretty soon you'll find that you are feeling more cheerful yourself."

"Say, Miss Long," Guy told her, "you're a cheerer-upper yourself. I feel better just talking to you. And will *you* pray for me to be a blessing instead of a blight to my fellow students?"

Still another explanation for failure may be ill health or some kind of unrevealed difficulty. Even if failure is due to incompetence or negligence, a compassionate attitude will be more helpful to the person than a condemnatory one.

Don was the last and most passive of several children. All of his brothers and sisters were aggressive and eager to make a success of their lives. Their father was proud of them and critical of his youngest boy, often comparing him unfavorably with them. But Don's mother praised him for anything she found to commend, and held out to him her anticipation of his improvement.

Eventually, it was learned that he had a hearing impairment that partly accounted for his low level of attainment. A glandular condition was also discovered which contributed to his poor performance. Along with remedial measures to correct these matters, Don was placed in a boarding school where he was not compared with his siblings and where he received more personal attention and encouragement. His mother regularly wrote letters calculated to inspirit and encourage him. In a few years' time he became a self-confident outgoing person who developed into a successful citizen.

Failure is sometimes due to lack of perseverance. Sometimes if one would just "keep on keeping on," the outcome might not be failure. This is where encouragement may be the crucial factor.

Barry loved basketball and had the height which could make him a valuable point maker but, try as he would, he could not toss the ball into the net. It always hit the rim and glanced away. His schoolmates made fun of him and told him he might as well give up, and he was just about to do so.

But his coach urged him to continue trying. "You'll get the knack of it any day now, Barry," he told the lad. "Keep on practicing and one of these days you'll hardly ever miss."

Years later, after Barry had become forward on a professional team, his boyhood coach liked to tell how his remark turned the tide of failure for the now-successful player.

Lack of foresight, conflict of interests, adverse economic conditions, and opposing attitudes all account for some of our failures. In many instances, encouragement at the right moment might have swung the pendulum the other way.

The basic element in discouragement caused by failure is loss of self esteem. If has been said that for every person who rates himself too highly there are dozens who feel they are worthless. Anyone who feels worthless, for whatever cause, needs a special brand of encouragement.

First we must identify ourselves with the failure by recognizing that everyone is a failure in some respect and, therefore, is not justified in being critical or superior because he has not failed in the *particular* area in which another has. The compassion of Christ must be ours in suffering with the one who has been defeated.

Next, it may be in order to remind him that he is an

individual of worth because God created him. Various Scriptures, such as Galatians 3:28-29, might be cited to support this fact.

It also might be helpful to mention that Jesus was considered a failure by his brothers and others, as John 7:3-5 points out. Peter tasted the gall of failure, and wept bitterly (Matthew 26:75). Thomas Edison was rated a failure by his schoolteacher. And others have been deemed failures in some area of life. In fact, *no* person escapes being a failure *somewhere* along the line, but this does not mean we are *total* failures as persons.

Perhaps it is fortunate that we fail sometimes. There is some profit to be reaped from every failure. Perhaps you can encourage someone by bringing this to his attention. Help him search for his *growth bonus* in what may be unfortunate circumstances.

Kay was a laboratory technician in a hospital which was closed during malpractice insurance negotiations. Because countless other hospitals in the state were closed for the same reason, she and dozens of others were out of employment. The market was glutted with persons of her skills, and she could not find another job. Being a child of God, she talked to her Heavenly Father about it.

One day as she was leafing through a Christian magazine, she happened to see the appeal of a well-known organization: "Your skills are needed overseas. . . ." She began to think of using her training in the Lord's service, instead of merely for her own profit.

After some preliminary training, Kay was ready for assignment abroad. By that time, the difficulties that had closed the hospitals had been overcome and most of them had reopened. A number of them communicated with her about joining their staff. Her happy commitment and testimony about her new assignment influenced several doctor friends to contribute to her support.

Present failure may be a stepping-stone to future success. No failure need be written off as permanent or irrevocable.

Even a business collapse may have some element of salvageability, as in the case of Fred. When he finished his military tour of overseas duty, he used the money he had accumulated to open a small business, which he had dreamed of doing all the time he was in the service. He looked forward to being his own boss and not having to take orders from anyone. But he soon discovered that he lacked the experience to make his business profitable. He couldn't sell the business and had to close up, having lost his investment and failed completely.

He had difficulty finding employment, but finally was hired in a field totally foreign to anything he had done before. He soon discovered, however, that it appealed to him, and he wished he had the knowledge to advance in that vocation.

His girl friend suggested that he see if GI benefits would enable him to get the training he wanted. By hard work and self-denial, along with government help, he was able to rise above the "failure" stigma. He gives his former girl friend, now his wife, credit for encouraging him in the right direction.

Instances such as this are assurance that what Paul said to the Romans (8:28) really is true: "We know that all things work together for good to them that love

God, to them who are the called according to his purpose." On the truth of this verse, Paul told believers, "In everything give thanks" (I Thessalonians 5:18).

Still another element that may be used for encouragement is the fact that, regardless of one's age or circumstances, God is favorable to his winning the victory, and will endue him for it.

Joshua was dispirited because of Israel's defeat at Ai. He felt that the situation was hopeless and he fell on his face in utter depression. But God told him to get up; then later, when Joshua was in better condition to profit by what God told him, He said, "Fear not, neither be thou dismayed..." (Joshua 8:1). Ultimately, Joshua enjoyed victory in place of defeat.

At one juncture in his life, Elijah despaired unto death. He told the Lord, "I've had enough. Take away my life" (I Kings 19:4b). Later, with his physical body renewed and a fresh assurance of God's enabling power, he resumed his activities as a prophet and voice for the Lord to Israel.

A cold dawn followed a hectic night for Peter, one that had involved physical danger, emotional tension, inward conflict, and deep disappointment. Now, as the cock crowed a second time, brash Peter realized his own utter failure, and he wept bitterly. Exactly as Jesus had predicted, he had denied his dear Lord three times. Very possibly, Peter had an impulse to hang himself, as did another failure, Judas.

For three days Peter must have brooded over his declension, reliving events, reviewing his denials, admitting to himself that he was indeed a colossal failure. But, on the third day, a light shone at the end of the tunnel. Some of the women who had been to the tomb brought the word that lifted his spirits and set him again on the course of the Lord's will for his life: ". . . tell his disciples *and Peter* that he goeth before you into Galilee" (Mark 16:7).

What a wonderful fact this illustrates! No matter what a dismal failure we are, or feel we are, or others say we are, Jesus understands and has compassion for us. He is always there, ready with: "Be of good cheer; I have overcome the world" (John 16:33).

Finally, let us note that, in lifting the spirits of one who has failed, we will not only help him but we will also do ourselves a favor. Martin Luther puts that thought this way, "If you help another to think well of himself, all the devils in Hell cannot make him think ill of you."

12
Smiles and Gestures Can Encourage

It is said, "A smile is the same in any language" — which makes it an effective introduction to spirit-lifting in any country. It flashes the message that one is amiably disposed and is transmitting good will in the other person's direction. That, in itself, is encouraging.

On the other hand, a frown or a scowl does exactly the reverse. It channels the idea of "Get ready for something unpleasant. Be prepared for disheartening developments." Immediately the one frowned upon begins to feel dismayed or dejected.

One's eyes can also initiate discouragement. If they express disapproval or criticism, the object of their glance or stare naturally becomes uncomfortable. If he doesn't know the reason for the unfavorable countenance, he is at least perplexed. If he suspects or knows what prompts it, he may become angry or dispirited. Then *his* face will reflect his reaction.

For instance, a child comes bounding into a room.

He is bubbling with joy and excitement. His father looks up from the troublesome report he is working on and frowns. His eyes flash annoyance at the interruption, and the corners of his mouth turn down in disapproval. He hasn't said a word, but already his little son's enthusiasm subsides, his shoulders droop, and he begins to back away. The boy has been discouraged from sharing his joy and, in fact, he is left feeling unsure as to whether it was even right for him to be joyous.

Another type of look which discourages is the "you poor worm" one. It brands the recipient as inferior, woefully lacking in something. No wonder it discourages him, particularly if he already has inferiority feelings.

Sometimes this look is not directed to the person involved, but detours past him to convey the message about him to another who is present. Perhaps it is accompanied by a supercilious lift of the eyebrow. We should pray for the person who purveys such negative attitudes, rather than permit him to dismay us. He brings himself under the condemnation of God, who says in Psalms 101:5b, ". . . him that hath an high look and a proud heart will not I suffer."

A refugee couple from Cuba were attending their first PTA meeting. Highly educated, professional people, they were determined to do all in their power to put their children on an equal footing with their American schoolmates, but they were obviously ill at ease.

Before the planned program was over, one of the older members caught the eye of the young Cuban mother and smiled at her. Slowly the other smiled back. The next time their eyes met, it was the Cuban who smiled first. Meantime the American had alerted her husband to the couple and reminded him of their need for encouragement. When he had opportunity, he nodded at the man, remembering they had been introduced at a service club meeting. The man's face relaxed into a pleased smile.

Gestures, as well as looks, can convey encouragement. An elderly man insisted on sitting in the back row in Sunday School although members had been exhorted to move up front.

When his daughter asked him why he did not do so, he said, "The members of other departments walk past that back pew as they go to their rooms. Often they pat my shoulder or squeeze my arm as they go past."

They were communicating encouragement to an old man.

A woman who had nightly seizures of violent coughing would often feel her husband's compassionate hand upon her. It said more eloquently than words, "I'm aware. I care. I'm praying for you." She often thought of the contrast between this encouraging gesture and the unsympathetic words of Job's wife relevant to his afflictions when she said, ". . . Curse God, and die" (Job 2:9).

Another woman was attending a dinner meeting of an organization to which she belonged. She noted the presence, second to her right, of a member who did not often attend the meetings and who resided in a home for senior citizens. The woman reached around the person between them and affectionately squeezed the shoulder of the elderly woman. That lady's eyes glowed as she commented, "Oh! It has been so long since anyone touched me."

Perhaps that spontaneous caress gave her fresh courage to return to an empty existence. Another person who had been encouraged in the same manner praised God for it in these words: "Dear God, thank you for the arm around my shoulder today. I surely needed it: A boost! A lift!"

If one cannot get near enough to another to personally transmit encouragement, perhaps a cordial wave of the hand will accomplish the same thing. In situations of closer proximity, a hearty handshake can be a means of encouraging a fellow citizen. Of course, the "dead fish" type of hand shaking does not do this. The handclasp must be firm enough to convey esteem and, thus, to cheer.

A seminary instructor in pastoral counseling told his students that it was important to touch a person as a means of conveying cordiality and compassion. Questioned about the propriety of it, he declared. "Everybody has enough skin somewhere that it's all right to touch." Actually, he was advising the type of gestures mentioned above.

It has been well said that "the hug that comforts, the arm around the shoulder that dissolves tension, the grip of a friendly hand — such human gestures are more profoundly rewarding than many of us realize."

Unfortunately, there are gestures which have an undesirable effect. A shrug may communicate superiority as a raised eyebrow does. To turn aside from encountering a person is a likely way of hurting or discouraging him.

What a shame it is that little gestures which require such slight effort on our part are not used more freely and frequently to encourage others! How timely the admonition in Colossians 3:12, "Put on therefore, as the elect of God, holy and beloved . . . mercies, kindness . . ." — and thus encourage others.

13
Spoken Words
Can Encourage

A widow struggling to rear her brood of children without a father was so despondent one Sunday morning that she was strongly tempted to absent herself from church. Nevertheless, a sense of duty to have her children in Sunday School impelled her to go.

As she entered her classroom, her teacher looked up, smiled at her and said, "Oh, Dorothy! How pretty you look this morning."

The mother testified afterward that this comment brightened her outlook and changed her mood. The day became one of joy instead of despair.

Such spirit lifting is possible for each of us. The very fact that we greet someone demonstrates an interest in him. It conveys to him that he is worthy of attention. One woman put it this way: "Until you came along, no one paid me any mind." What a challenge that is to us to gaze concernedly at the people around us and raise the self-esteem of someone who is being overlooked ·

If circumstances do not permit conversation, one can always offer a pleasant nod of recognition. Too many times, however, it is not a lack of opportunity, but a lack of initiative, that is responsible for failure. Often we choose to encircle ourselves with those at the center rather than to cultivate friendships with those on the fringes. Unfortunately, this is as true at Christian as at secular gatherings.

Due to this type of situation, some churches are considered unfriendly. It is a discouraging experience for one to go to a service and suffer indifferent glances or a few lukewarm greetings. Even the pastor's "God bless you" at the door may seem perfunctory and devoid of personal interest.

In contrast, a visitor in another type of church was cheered by the warmth and friendliness with which he was greeted. He even received an invitation to go home to dinner with one couple who talked to him.

A group of women on their way to a meeting stopped at a funeral home where the body of the husband of one of their members lay in state. There they greeted the widow and offered their condolences. Later she wrote, "Your presence that evening gave me courage to face the future. I felt the love of God shining through my sorrow."

That is the way God meant it to be. Singly or collectively, He expects His children to offer encouragement. And the spoken word is one means of doing it.

A couple entered a Christian bookstore abroad. The man who waited on them was not aware of it, but the couple were so depressed that they planned to commit suicide. The bookseller witnessed to them of the love of

God and gave them a booklet to read that transformed their lives. Not until they wrote back and reported it did the man know how he had had a part in lifting their spirits.

Another unusual opportunity for encouragement occurred in a car in which three women were riding to a cemetery. Two of them were depressed because their husbands did not know the Lord. The third woman told them of the experience of a friend who won her husband to Christ after twenty years of life and lip witness. When they parted, one of the ladies said to her, "You have been a real encouragement to me today."

A sincere and appropriate compliment is nearly always a spirit lifter. At the risk of being repetitious, we point out that there are many areas where a compliment can be offered: appearance, conduct, accomplishments, and potentialities. Most of us are quick to note items to criticize. From now on, let's look for items to praise.

Compliments and appreciation are two sides of a coin. Appreciation may motivate the expression of a compliment. Yet there is something deeper to appreciation, because it is possible to sincerely compliment one without being fully appreciative.

The word *appreciate* has the same root as the word "appraise." The latter means *to place a value on, to estimate its worth.* Appraise, has no emotional overtones. Appreciate carries with it the connotation of warmth of feeling. So, when we appreciate someone we are recognizing their worth in a warm or loving manner. Almost always, therefore, appreciation buoys the spirits.

Whom have you appreciated today or this week,

either in respect to what he is or to what he does? Members of your family? The bus driver? The service station operator? The mail man? A civic official? A customer? A clerk? Your boss?

A pastor answered his phone one day to hear a woman at the other end of the line say, "I was studying the Sunday School lesson and learned that Barnabas means *encourager*. I can't be a Barnabas because I'm a female, but I *can* tell you how much we appreciate your good sermons, your ready sympathy and your warm willingness to be of help."

That preacher testified that her conversation put him on cloud nine for the rest of the day. How long has it been since you conveyed appreciation of some sort for your spiritual leader?

Too often we are careless about expressing the appreciation that mere etiquette calls for. Newlyweds receive gifts, staff workers receive gratuities, neighbors accept favors, and commercial enterprises are awarded business without ever an acknowledgement of gratitude. The fact that, in any of the foregoing incidents, the deed might have been withheld with some sort of loss to the beneficiary is proof that it constituted a reason for appreciation.

A businessman customarily gave a Christmas bonus to each of his employees. Because they regularly received a salary commensurate with their services, they were not justified in feeling that they "had it coming." While some of them graciously thanked him for the bonus, others never mentioned it. Wouldn't that discourage him? And conversely, wouldn't appreciation encourage him to continue giving the bonus?

Another means of encouraging downhearted

persons with a spoken word is by relaying assurances to them. Their discouragement may be due to fear, apprehension, lack of foreknowledge, or inexperience. Often a word can be spoken which will acquaint them with unknown facts or will allay their fears.

A man who had always enjoyed good health was suddenly confronted with the necessity of hospitalization for surgery. A friend, who surmised his situation, visited him and casually relayed information on the medical procedures that would be involved. He reported them in an offhand manner, all of which served to reassure the sick man.

Many times the best possible way to convey assurance is by quoting pertinent Scriptures. There is a Biblical encouragement for every situation, and if one can be a purveyor of its good news, the inevitable result will be the lifting of depression.

A woman who was obsessed with fear testifies that a sign on a church which she passed became a factor in her release from the recurrent phobia which gripped her. The sign read: "The name of the Lord is a strong tower; the righteous runneth into it, and is safe" (Proverbs 18:10).

Casual conversation may be the means by which one's spirits are lifted. A businessman stopped at a hamburger shop for a snack. There he ran into two Christian friends. They exchanged greetings and continued talking after being served. The couple rejoiced at all the Lord had done and was doing as they recalled past experiences in a local church. (It is timely to note here that praise and thanksgiving are spirit lifters of an infectious nature.)

Presently, as the man rose to leave he told his

friends, "I had a bad experience with a client just before coming here; consequently, I was feeling quite depressed. Our visit has given me encouragement. It has made my day."

In another instance, from his office window the president of a Christian college could see a young married student-preacher wearing a dejected look. The older man opened the window and called out, "Rod, lift your chin. Remember—you're a child of the King." The friendly, valid admonition brightened the man's outlook.

Similarly, this day or this week, you may have an opportunity to "make" someone's day, to dissipate his gloom, and set his heart singing. Are you ready and watching for it?

14
Written Words
Can Encourage

Each of the following letter excerpts was a spirit lifter to the one who received it.

"You came and you went. You brought the fragrance of Heaven and you left an abiding enrichment amongst us, and I thank God for sending you. I thank God for your presence, and I thank God for His blessing in answer to your continuing prayers. You are very dear to me personally; you are more dear to the Saviour, and you mean much for the Kingdom of God."

"I praise the Lord for bringing you into my life, and the challenge you have been and are to me to fully and completely trust Christ for everything."

"Certainly you are spreading sunshine and inspiration, and brightening the corner where you are for those who drop in on you. May the Lord continue to bless you and use you as you carry on your cheery witness for Him."

"I am thankful for the strength and encouragement

received from the times I was with you. . . . You are a treasured friend indeed; your letters are a real comfort and encouragement to me."

"Sometimes things happen to brighten our days, and now and then something that brightens our life. Such was your card and note. It was thoughtful of you to send it, and it was also a happy surprise. . . . You have been such a source of comfort and consolation to me over the past several years. I want you to know the help you have been to me."

"You'll never know how you have influenced my life and I shall never cease to be grateful. . . . I love you so much and feel so indebted to you. You've meant so much in my life and your prayers are so effective. I attribute, in a large measure, to your effectual fervent prayers that avail so much, my job and what it has meant."

"Thank you for the challenge your life has given me. I want you to know that you definitely have had dividends on your prayer life. I thank God for your life of dedication and inspiration. . . . The last check I had was for $21, and because of you, the Lord will get it all."

"Now, if I might deviate from business for a moment. I told my Bible Class on Sunday about the fine trip we had and about the nice Christian people we met, how your Christianity seems to effervesce, how you prayed aloud at the table and how your enthusiasm for Christ overflowed. You both seem to radiate a feeling of Christian love and contentment and a faith that is refreshingly contagious. You reflect the appreciation of the Lord's blessings."

"I can never thank God enough for your help to me in

these dark hours. . . . What a joy to my heart your letter brought. I cried to think I had such a wonderful friend that would pray for me each day. It's a blessing from God to know you wonderful people and to really know someone cares for us with the love of God and will pray when they say they will."

None of these letters were literary efforts; they were simply sincere expressions of appreciation for something about the person or ministry of the one addressed. Because letters can do so much for others and cost as little as they do, one wonders why so many people loathe writing them, or put off writing them indefinitely, thus failing to cheer up a friend when they might.

One need not carry on a frequent correspondence in order to be a spirit lifter. Timeliness, rather than number or length of letters, is most apt to be their encouraging aspect. Has there been illness or a bereavement? Has a son or daughter gone away to school or the military or married and left home? Mail may be a bright spot in days that seem longer because of the departure.

Or there may have been other trials, such as a business slump, a car wreck, a robbery—any situation that might depress one is the occasion for writing a note of encouragement. Perhaps one will not even mention the misfortune, but will simply convey that he is mindful and sympathetic to the person's hardships.

There are greeting cards for practically any circumstance in which one might be involved. Some depict sincere emotion; others offer a bit of satire or humor. They are better than silence, but even their use is enhanced if one pens a personal sentence or two before signing them.

One may find a poem or paragraph to clip and post to a friend who has cause for the blues. Or sometimes one reads an item in a local or regional paper recounting some achievement of a friend. That person may glow if you clip the item and send it to him with a note of congratulations. (He may be glad to have an extra copy of it, too.)

If one is sensitive to the Spirit's leading, he may communicate cheer without even being aware of it, until he is told later that there was a special need for encouragement.

A Christian loaned a book which had been a blessing to her to a friend, not knowing of a particular need that existed in the recipient's life. The book proved to be a great encouragement to the one to whom it was loaned, because it dealt with a problem which existed in her family at that very time.

One must always be mindful that the most powerful written word he can use to convey encouragement is the Word of God. The Bible contains encouragement for every person in whatever disheartening situation he may find himself.

The Gideons, the non-denominational, international organization of evangelical Christian business and professional men, have dedicated themselves to making the Scriptures available to the public. They place Bibles in motels, hotels, hospitals, penal institutions, on trains and planes, in the waiting rooms of doctors and dentists, and elsewhere.

On the opening flyleaf of the Bibles a section is titled, "Help in Time of Need." It lists various conditions under which one might be disheartened. Opposite each of these items appears the location of a Bible passage which might impart encouragement to the reader. The page on which it is found is listed for ready reference. As a result of the availability of this help, there is documented evidence that many despondent persons who intended to commit suicide have received courage to go forward.

The Gideon magazine reports one such instance. A woman who was touring New Zealand, but who was deeply depressed, decided to end her life by throwing herself in front of a bus or by jumping into the harbor. She was waiting in a motel room for nightfall before carrying out her intentions. Meanwhile, she picked up a Bible which had been placed on the dresser by the Gideons. There, in that motel room, she was transformed into a child of God. Encouraged by God, she returned to her home and was reunited with her husband, who later found the same source of assurance she had found.

There are many other Christian organizations which get the Word into the hands of people who need spiritual help and encouragement. As we give them our support and prayer help we can share in their ministry of lifting spirits in places abroad as well as in our own country. What a privilege!

15
Actions Can
Encourage

It was "blue Monday" for Sue, so when her children requested that they go visit a friend, she consented, not knowing what the Lord had in store for her. Arriving at the friend's home, the two mothers, both of them children of God, engaged in conversation while the children played together.

The hostess was bubbling over with joy for the Lord's goodness and how He had been working in her family's life. Her enthusiasm was contagious and served to lift the spirits of her visitor so that she, too, began to rejoice.

Often the transaction would have taken place the other way. The one doing the visiting would have ministered encouragement to the one being visited. Either way, the act of visiting may lift the depression someone is experiencing.

A telephone call can also be the means of dissipating depression. Lynn was despondent about a matter that had arisen in connection with their business. She telephoned another child of God who cited helpful Scriptures to her and prayed over the telephone with her. It boosted her morale immeasurably.

Valerie was experiencing a case of the "blahs." Even though she was a child of God, the joy of it had waned. Dispiritedly, she called a friend to check on some little matter. The friend sensed her caller's discouragement and gave her such a rousing testimony to God's wonders and sufficiency that Valerie hung up delivered from her boredom.

In some communities cheering by telephone is an organized activity. By arrangement, volunteers daily call certain persons who dwell alone to let them know someone cares and seeks to encourage them.

One church runs a newspaper ad inviting "sick, desperate, and depressed people" to phone a given number. When one does, a gentle, reassuring voice quotes comforting Scriptures and prays for the caller. Many persons have taken fresh courage from such conversations.

Again, a personal contact may be the channel of encouragement. Frank had had disquieting news from his doctor and was brooding somewhat over it when a friend entered his office and invited him to go to coffee. Frank consented, and over the table, his host shared his Bible-based optimism. Frank had an improved attitude when he returned to his desk.

Another means of heartening those who are down-cast may be by one's example. A businessman, who had seen the scheming, cheating side of human nature for years as a wholesale produce distributor, doubted that there was a good man to be found.

Sunday after Sunday the man who lived across the

street from the businessman could be seen leaving his house with his Bible under his arm as he headed for Sunday School and church. The cynic discovered that this neighbor's life measured up to his verbal profession of faith. Encouraged by the man's example, the produce distributor also began attending services. In the course of time, he became a believer and faithful church worker.

An elderly lady who had lost her sight still spread cheer to others. She managed to sign cards, which friends addressed for her. She spent much of her time telephoning encouragement to those going through trials. Moreover, in lifting the spirits of others, she lifted her own.

One Christian couple invest themselves in the ministry of encouragement by baby-sitting occasionally for mothers who have too tight a budget to afford a paid sitter. Their selfless act gives cheer to one for whom continual confinement could be discouraging. They have kept company with elderly persons on the same basis: to relieve the one who is usually confined with them, and thus impart cheer to him or her.

The Suttons invited a senior citizen and his wife to their home for dinner. The couple had felt dreary because they were no longer able to engage in some activities they had previously enjoyed. The fact that someone was interested enough to entertain them encouraged them. The change of environment and sharing a bit in the lives of others was also helpful to them.

Hospitality, whether the simplest and most casual or on a more expansive scale, is usually a means of spirit lifting. One who had benefited from hospitality wrote back saying:

"Thank you for the many 'memory gems' we have tucked away to bring out from time to time and thus recall those happy days in your company. Most of all we say thank you for your spiritual depth, our prayer time, and sweet fellowship in Him. Thanks for sharing some of yourselves with us."

Another form of action which mediated encouragement was that of a pastor's wife who gives this report about encouraging a musician who lacked self-confidence:

"I played the piano for years because there was no one else to play, but during those years I knew of one who played beautifully. She played with a touch I can never achieve, and correctly, and with a keen understanding of music. Louise didn't attend church much for quite some time, but after she commenced coming to church regularly I told her many times how much I enjoyed her playing and ability. I also told her that I looked forward to her taking over all the playing. When special skill was needed, I asked for Louise. When the revival meetings came along, if I thought they would be a blessing to her, I would ask her to play for the meetings. As a result, Louise grew spiritually. Soon she began to play for the Sunday morning service, and also began teaching in Sunday School."

This same woman also reports that when the girls of the church began playing the piano well enough for congregational singing, she would ask them to play. She was prompted to do this because she remembered that when she was learning to play it was very helpful to her to play for church. Perhaps this encouragement of neophyte musicians accounts for the fact that one of the girls went on to the state university to major in music.

Another instance of that type of encouragement sprang from the need for a Sunday School teacher for teenage girls. When a young mother's baby had become old enough for her to undertake such a class, the pastor's wife started telling her that she wished the girls had her for a teacher. She also told a key person on the nominating committee that this woman would be great for the girls. The young mother was enlisted for the position and continued for a number of years doing a great job because she taught with her life as well as her words.

Needless to point out, a gift is often a means of buoying up low spirits. It need not have a great monetary value. Its *real* value is in its message that the recipient is accepted and esteemed. Or its timeliness in meeting a need may be the factor that cheers up the recipient rather than its price tag.

A hostess who did not live near a store and had not had time to do any baking, was thrilled when a guest brought some cookies she had made.

Sharing from one's abundance with those living on marginal incomes can certainly raise their spirits. A wheelchair Christain and her elderly mother were beneficiaries of this kind of encouragement. The following letter betokened their level of joy:

Dear Good Neighbors:
          Sometimes we wonder what we've done to merit such kindness as you folks have shown us. Nothing we've done— just that you folks have such splendid

Christian character. We appreciate every single thing more than words can express.

Your habit of often saying, "Let's have a word of prayer" tops the list. That is a spiritual uplift that we need. Then you've brought gifts so often: fruit, flowers, candy, cake, fish; oh-so-good milk and eggs, and I mustn't forget the magazines. We think you people are true examples of Christians in action.

May God bless you richly, and we know many others are saying the same thing. We covet your prayers, now and always, and we look forward to more prayers together in our home.

Sincerely,

Bessie and her mother

Whether one's gift is one of self only, or of substance also, under God it can be a source of encouragement to a fellowman.

16
The Rewards of
Spirit Lifting

Whatever we do, ". . . it is for your cause. For the love of Christ constraineth us" (II Corinthians 5:13-14a).

Any selfish motive for seeking to lift another's spirits will render the work useless. Such an effort may categorize us as despised do-gooders instead of channels of blessing. Only when love prompts a sincere desire to be of help does our ministry become effective.

Often under such circumstances it can be unpremeditatively, even unconsciously, effective. Of such a helper a woman wrote, "I think so often of you and your kindness to all; perhaps you are unaware of it, but you have a Christlike manner at all times that touches one and lingers. Oh, that we had more Christians like that!"

In Matthew 6:2 and 3, Christ condemned those whose motives were selfish: "Therefore when thou doest thine alms, do not sound a trumpet before thee, as the hypocrites do in the synagogues and in the streets, that they may have glory of men. Verily I say unto you, They have their reward. But when thou doest alms, let not thy left hand know what thy right hand doeth."

Our impulses for spirit lifting are to be without fanfare or publicity. Then our efforts will bless the recipient and bring reward to the spirit lifter. And make no mistake, such rewards are gratifying.

Lifting the spirit of another adds a new dimension to one's own life. In this respect one testified, "There are so many things I cannot do and when I try, I only fail. It is most frustrating. Nevertheless, the Lord has graciously let me see many results of my giving encouragement here and there, making a suggestion now and then with beautiful outcome. Sometimes it is only to happily give an explanation that relieves a sticky situation and brings peace instead of ill will. It truly is a joy to see bad attitudes melt away when love moves in with gentle understanding."

This quotation points up another important aspect: the ministry of spirit lifting can become a customary way of life. One can make it a habit to note and appreciate positive, instead of negative, characteristics. One can look for items to compliment instead of criticize. One can be alert for situations to appreciate instead of depreciate.

Surprising as it may seem, when one cultivates this attitude, his own personality, and even his health, may be improved by it. What better reward could one have than that? Clyde Narramore, a noted Christian psychologist, makes this recommendation: "If you are rather negative, start making a point of complimenting people and encouraging them regularly."

It goes without saying that this earns the esteem of the one who is encouraged. One expressed his appreciation thus: "I keep thinking of how greatly blessed are we who are your friends, those who have been privileged to know and love you, and share Christian fellowship with you. You touched such an important part of our lives and helped us in so many ways."

Another testified: "How we do love you two beautiful Christians! We thank God each and every day for you and for sending you our way."

Often a husband and wife can join forces to be a team of encouragers. What one overlooks, the other may see. What might sound like flattery if said by one person can be divided between the two with a cheer-up effect. The very fact that a husband and wife engage together in such a ministry may encourage another. Such a one wrote: "I just praise the Lord for having known such precious Christians as you. You both have done so many wonderful things for the Lord." Another wrote, "Thank you for just being you and for giving such a wonderful witness. We appreciate both of you so much." Still another testified, "I never cease to be amazed at how efficiently you folks handle all the people who pass your way, how you make each one feel very special and manage to show each a good time. Praise the Lord for your willingness to be involved with people."

David Dunn, author of *Try Giving yourself Away,* says, "When I'm worried or generally low in spirits, a conscious effort to give myself away works wonders."

The greatest reward of all may be God's "well done." Referring to deeds of encouragement, Christ declared, "Come, ye blessed of my Father, inherit the kingdom prepared for you from the foundation of the world," because, He said, ". . . as ye have done it unto one of the least of these . . . ye have done it unto me" (Matthew 25:34, 40).

What greater encouragement could there be to the spirit lifter than this promise from the Saviour?

17
Everyone Can Encourage Some-one Somewhere

A member of the military stationed in the Orient encountered a very old man struggling under a terrific load. He couldn't speak the language, but he motioned to the old man to set down his burden. With obvious fear of some mistreatment which might occur, the native complied.

The soldier took off his belt, clasped it around the bundle, then found a stick he could thrust under the strap. He gripped one end of the stick and motioned to the old fellow to take the other end, so that the weight was divided between them. Grinning delightedly, the elderly man led the way to his destination. Upon arriving, he bowed over and over to express his appreciation.

There isn't anywhere on earth that one cannot be a spirit lifter because the need is universal. Everywhere there is someone who needs some kind of encouragement. The field for this ministry is not only worldwide; there are many and varied possibilities as to how the encouragement may be channeled. Moreover, a noteworthy aspect of spirit lifting is that there is no tax or time schedule on it. Any time, any day, any season, in any place—at home or abroad, at work or play or school, at church or club meeting—you can engage in spirit lifting.

Picture a gardener irrigating his plot. He has channeled life-giving water to all of it except one little plant way over in the corner. It is languishing because of the lack. The gardener knows that if he just had one more piece of pipe he could reach it to transform it from a wilting bit of flora to an erect, thriving piece of vegetation.

So it is with the Master Gardener. Because He chooses to minister through human beings, He needs many lengths of pipe in order to bless persons here, there, and everywhere. In the area where you are there is a drooping person who needs God's ministry of encouragement. Will you be that extra piece of pipe through which He can channel His cheer?

The exciting part about spirit lifting is that it can surmont all barriers—age, sex, nationality, social class. To evidence interest and concern is to start the melting of barriers. Gestures of goodwill *by* enough people *to* enough persons can overcome ill will and hostility populationwise, but it has to begin with you and me on a person-to-person basis. Christ Himself set the example. As a spirit lifter, He voiced: "In the world ye shall have tribulation; but be of good cheer; I have overcome the world" (John 16:33).

With Him as your partner and the Holy Spirit as your guide, today—*now*—wherever you are
BE A SPIRIT LIFTER.